Subaru Impreza

by Julie Wilson

Acknowledgements

Cover design: Oliver Heath, Rafters Design

Photographs © Subaru (UK) Limited

First published in Great Britain by Axis Education Ltd

ISBN 1-84618-016-3

Axis Education
PO Box 459
Shrewsbury
SY4 4WZ

Email: enquiries@axiseducation.co.uk

www.axiseducation.co.uk

The design of the Subaru Impreza brings to mind an action scene – high speed handbrake turns whilst tearing along dirt tracks in a mud-splattered car. It's not surprising, then, that this car was originally made famous on the World Rally Championship (WRC) circuit. Whichever model you're looking at, the Impreza is a mixture of style and aggression.

Subaru itself has a great reputation for car making. With new models coming out all the time, their features and performance are always being improved. With improvements comes desire, especially from enthusiasts, and each Impreza model has caused a small rumble among the Subaru faithful for whom 'Scoobies' are the ultimate.

Indeed, with the Impreza, they've designed a car with attitude. It's easy to see why you'd be tempted to climb into one at the first opportunity and burn up the nearest motorway.

Subaru is improving its models all the time.

WR1

In celebration of winning the 2003 WRC Driver's Title, Subaru brought out the Impreza WRX STi limited edition – the WR1. This is the fastest and most powerful Impreza ever. Only 500 were made, a sure sign of its exclusivity in the world of car manufacturing.

Its starting price at the time of manufacture was around £29,000, which made it the most expensive Subaru apart from the WRC itself. With so few made and at that cost, the WR1 *should* be special!

Petter Solberg with the winning Subaru in 2003.

You can't mistake a WR1 when you see it. There is only one colour to choose from: Ice Blue Metallic. This is understandable with a limited edition – more than one shade would take away something of its individual superiority. A colour like Ice Blue Metallic speaks for itself, suggesting that anyone driving this car may need to have some street cred to do so.

The value of street cred is clear when an Impreza passes you on the road. Gold alloy wheels and a high-rise spoiler make it obvious that this machine means business.

The designers have added driving lamps below the headlights and stainless steel mesh grille at the front. There are collapsible windscreen wipers, colour-coded bumpers, door handles and mirrors. Add these to the aluminium bonnet and your next move has got to be to get inside and check out what the interior has to offer.

The limited edition WR1.

As promised by the style of the WR1's exterior, the inside is car heaven.

Aluminium pedals, bucket seats and electric windows with tinted glass remind you that this is a sports car, as if you needed such a reminder. The car has semi-automatic air conditioning, a useful tool in a high performance vehicle. For safety, there are driver and front passenger airbags.

For added comfort, you can adjust the height and tilt of the driver's seat. To add to the feeling of high-speed luxury, there is a centre visor, a chromed handbrake button, a four-speaker CD system, map reading spotlights and front and centre console cup holders. The only question left is – where's the coffee maker?

Where's the coffee maker?

For Scoobies, the Impreza is a performance vehicle. However, with the WR1, Subaru shows that style is as important as performance.

Each vehicle has WR1 badging on the side and all are individually numbered.

The carpet mats and gear knob are branded and even the tax disc holder is engraved with the special edition number. Another special edition touch is that the gear knob and steering wheel are covered in leather with red stitching.

Perhaps £29,000 is a small price to pay for something that may be worth a great deal more in years to come.

Style is as important as performance for Subaru.

With speed-sensitive power steering and all-wheel drive technology, drivers are in control. There is a switch next to the handbrake that allows you to change power between the front and rear wheels, giving ultimate control at high speed, even around corners and tight bends. That's the sort of handling that makes you feel not only safe, but powerful.

The WR1 is no slouch, either. It can go from 0 to 62mph (0 to 100kmh) in just 4.25 seconds and 0 to 100mph (0 to 160kmh) in 10.67 seconds. Road tests have shown that it covers a quarter of a mile in only 12.8 seconds. If you can find somewhere legal (and safe) to do it, you can race to a top speed of 155mph (249kmh).

Somehow it becomes obvious that the basics of this car are in racing technology. As enjoyable to drive around built-up areas as the open road or racetrack, you can put this car wherever you want it. You're the boss.

With such great handling, you feel completely in control.

WXR STi

In 1998, Subaru Technica International (STi) in Japan decided to build a limited run of world rally replicas. They made 400. Within 72 hours of going on sale, there were none left.

In response to this amazing level of interest, Subaru started production of the STi. It must be the similarities to the WRC car that make it so popular. After all, if you'd always wanted to drive a world championship rally car, the STi would be a very strong substitute.

The grille, the badging, a high-riding boot spoiler and deep, square front bumper all serve to make it stand out from the crowd. The effect is heightened by the reappearance of the gold-coloured wheels, this time with 10 spokes. According to Subaru drivers, the STi's performance does not let its appearance down.

The WRX STi, where road car meets rally car.

The reputation of the STi is impressive. The latest model has had improvements that make a fantastic drive even better. They show the manufacturer's resolve to keep the STi at the forefront of modern performance know-how.

Improvements to the steering have resulted in more accuracy and less kick-back on bumpy roads or hard cornering. It reacts to the road surface and adapts accordingly, making the driver feel totally in control. Luckily, it also reacts positively to the driver who wants to change direction in a hurry!

You're in control with this car.

Put it where you want it. You're the boss.

The inside of the STi has been created to remind drivers that they are in a Subaru, and the Subaru is a car to be reckoned with.

Blue suede-effect seats with the STi logo sit neatly beside a steering wheel, gear knob and handbrake again decorated with smart red stitching. The doors are covered with a cloth trim and the air conditioning controls are shaped like diamonds. Along with the radio controls, they are easy to use when on the road. As a slight difference from the norm, UK models are fitted with an alarm/immobiliser and a satellite tracking system.

Surprisingly for a sports car, there is plenty of room for four people. The back seats are roomy enough for two more adults and there's a decent-sized boot to take some baggage. You can take the family out and show off while you're doing it!

There is enough room inside for the family and the dog!

With the inside of the WRX STi Impreza, the company has created a heady mix of stylish sports chic and echoes of the high-octane experience you're going to enjoy once you're on the highway. Imagine the excitement when you're testing the open road from an interior that looks and feels as smart as the exterior.

It's a good job then, that the STi's sports seats fulfil their promises and provide comfort and stability when taking those sharp corners.

The stylish interior of the WRX STi lets you know you're in for an exciting ride.

There's no looking back once you're on that highway.

The WRX STi can reach a top speed of 148mph (238kmh) and get from 0 to 62mph (0 to 100kmh) in just 5.2 seconds. Granted, that's a bit slower than the WR1 but it's a quicker mover than the average family saloon.

In fact, this car's speed is misleading. If you're tempted to put your foot down after a careful drive through a speed camera area, you'll probably find yourself behind with your gear changes and have to race through them to keep up.

Once you've got used to its rocket-like acceleration, it's a matter of small steering movements around bends and painless gear changes to get you from A to B. The easy gear shifting and sensitive steering make this car fast, stylish and fun to drive. The control provided by the four-wheel drive makes you trust this car to keep you on the road no matter how fast you're going. If you're not careful, though, you'll be speeding at over 100mph (160kmh) without realising.

For rounding bends, just touching the brake beforehand keeps the car where you want it. Coming to a complete halt requires only a little more force.

As a driving experience, it's pretty impressive.

It's easy to go too fast without realising it in the WRX STi.

Find somewhere safe (and legal) to do it and you can reach 148mph (238kmh).

GX Sport

For people who love the brand but can't pay upwards of £24,000 for their favourite car, the more standard GX Sport is available. This is a good idea. When you're a world famous car manufacturer whose reputation rests on your design of championship rally cars, and road cars that look like rally cars, why not produce a model that boy racers can afford? The GX may be cheaper, but it still carries the spirit of the racetrack.

Featuring Subaru's trademark four-wheel drive system, the GX Sport has all of the handling, road holding, performance and typical engine sound expected of an Impreza.

There are three models: the 1.6 TS, the 2.0 GX and the WRX. All three are available as either a four-door saloon or a five-door sports wagon. The 2.0-litre model is also available with an automatic gearbox.

The GX Sport has the distinctive features of a performance Subaru at half the price.

Each model is kitted out with four electric windows, mirrors with power adjustment and a single-slot CD player. The air-conditioning and radio controls are easy to use on the move.

Comfort is good, too, even with the turbo's bolstered sports seats. You also get those unmistakable Subaru alloy wheels, but not in gold!

You may think that the trademark features of the Subaru are a magnet to thieves. Thankfully, the GX has top-notch security features. There are less reported break-ins now that later models are fitted with deadlocks and shielded door locks. Keyless entry central locking and a Category One alarm/immobiliser make this car a tough nut to crack.

With bolstered seats and alloy wheels, you'll think you're in a WR1.

The GX package is well in keeping with the Impreza's sporty character. Revving the engine creates a familiar 'thrum' before building up to fast acceleration. Perhaps it isn't the STi, but it provides the driver with a smooth ride – there's decent poke from the engine and awesome overtaking ability (if you have the turbo-charged version).

Subaru has done a good job with both the ride and the handling of the GX. This Impreza manages to grip the ground over humps and dips and stays flat through bends, even in dangerous conditions. Again, it doesn't matter that the GX costs thousands of pounds less than the STi. Its performance and make-up show how Subaru will go all out to produce a vehicle that thinks it's a rally car.

If your thing is style, speed and attitude at an affordable price, what more could you want?

The GX Sport thinks it's a rally car. It could be right.

The WRC

Finally, the real thing!

If you hear the names Colin McRae, Richard Burns and Petter Solberg and know who they are, chances are you'll know something about the World Rally Championship (WRC). The Subaru World Rally Team was the first to launch a World Rally Car and, at the 1997 Monte Carlo Rally, the first to win with the new concept that currently dominates the sport.

You might also know that between 1993 and the beginning of 2004, the Subaru team scored 38 WRC wins. The Subaru trademarks of a horizontally opposed engine and full-time all-wheel drive combine to make a winning formula that crosses directly from forest track to highway. It has earned a strong reputation on rallies all around the world and is truly an icon of modern motor sport.

On the outside, both road and rally Imprezas share the same aggressive styling. The latest WRC, introduced in 2004, has a body shell that is lighter and stiffer than its predecessor of 2003. Its body panels are made of carbon fibre to make it as light as possible. Under the bonnet, the two-litre boxer engine now has improved turbo and exhaust systems. These boost its power and driveability.

The WRC – an icon of modern motor sport.

The WRC is a state-of-the art world rally car.

Purpose-built to WRC regulations, it costs around $500,000, a reasonable price tag when you remember that the WRC is the second most prestigious motor sport in the world (behind Formula 1). Manufacturers and sponsors are prepared to spend millions of dollars in order to win in this sport. If regulations change at any time, the entire vehicle is taken apart and rebuilt to fit exact specifications.

Side by side – the WRC and WRX STi.

There is much affection for these cars amongst the Subaru faithful. The 72-hour sell-out in 1998 of the 400 WRX STi limited run says it all, really. That sporty, fighter shape and powerful performance appeals to people who want a road car that feels and looks as if it has been built with the same thinking as that of a WRC racer.

Something else that pleases Scoobie followers is that there is always something to talk about, as Subaru is continually designing and developing its models. The Impreza of this year is not as advanced, comfortable, powerful and stylish as that of next year, and so on for years to come. The brand will go on improving because Subaru puts superior driving performance at the top of its priorities.

In 2004, the Subaru World Rally Team was made up of nearly 200 dedicated and skilled individuals. All of these were working towards the same single goal – winning. This insistence on getting it right travels right through Subaru's designs, from World Rally racers, limited editions and high performance road cars down to the more affordable and family-friendly GX – a sign of how committed the company is to its success and reputation.

The WR1. A limited edition. A Subaru.

Technical specification – Subaru Impreza

Make	Subaru
Model	Impreza WRX STi
Engine size	1994cc
Top speed	148 mph (238kmh)
Acceleration	0–62 mph (0–100kmh) in 5.5 seconds
Fuel tank capacity	60 litres
Price	£26,000
Weight	1880kg
Transmission	6-speed manual
Wheelbase	2540mm
Tyres	225/45 R17

Glossary

acceleration	how fast the car speeds up
alloy wheels	stylish wheels made of a blend of metals and bigger in size than standard wheels
all-wheel drive technology	where the power and control is in all four wheels
auto clutch manual	a type of gear transmission
badging	the marking of the car with the Subaru logo
bolstered	strengthened, reinforced
boxer engine	an engine design based on the movement of the pistons
carbon fibre	a high strength material now used more and more in industry
cc (cubic centimeters)	a measure of engine capacity
central-locking	locking the car from the driver's door
centre console cup holders	cup holders in the area between the seats and below the dashboard
centre visor	a sun shade in the centre of the windscreen
chrome	made of chrome, a shiny, hard metal
collapsible	will fold down when not in use
distinctive	noticeable, special
heightened	emphasized, made sharper
high rise spoiler	A metal strip that helps control airflow around the car. It is called a spoiler because it 'spoils' the normal airflow over the car.
high-octane	exhilarating, high-power
horizontally opposed engine	engine design where the cylinders are placed horizontally opposite each other and the whole engine lies flat

icon	an idol, something or someone you look up to
kick-back	jerks made by the steering when going over bumps and round tight corners
limited edition	when only a small number of a model is produced
mesh grilles	the framework at the front of the car.
poke	slang for 'power'
predecessor	the one before
purpose built	built for a specific purpose
replicas	direct copies
saloon	a four-door car
satellite tracking system	a computer system that can tell you how to get from A to B
Scoobies	the name Subaru enthusiasts give to the cars
slouch	a lazy person
speed-sensitive power steering	steering that reacts to the speed of the car
spokes	rods from the centre of the wheels to the rim
sponsors	people and businesses who pay a lot of money to finance a project with the aim of getting their name advertised
street cred	street credibility, being cool, acceptance from other 'trendies'
transmission	another word for gearbox
turbo	where exhaust gas boosts engine power
turbo-charged	where the engine power is boosted by exhaust gas